All Is Not Lost

*They Didn't Kill Me, They Just Propelled
Me to My Destiny*

TANYA KIDD

ISBN 978-1-64114-072-0 (paperback)
ISBN 978-1-64114-073-7 (digital)

Christian Faith Publishing, Inc.
832 Park Avenue
Meadville, PA 16335
www.christianfaithpublishing.com

Printed in the United States of America

Contents

Acknowledgments 5

Introduction...7

1. The Battle Begins 11

2. The Foundation Is Laid...13

3. Innocence Lost..16

4. Hopelessness 19

5. Determination..21

6. My Faith Tested...23

7. Taking Charge of My Life 26

8. Shattered Dreams..28

9. Depression Takes Over 30

10. Confusion 32

11. Lost..36

12. Freedom..40

13. Torn 44

14. Out of Control..48

15. Self-Realization 52

16. Getting on Track 60

17. Acceptance 62

Acknowledgments

I would like to dedicate this book to my God Lord Jehovah, without whom I could do nothing or be anything. I owe everything to him. To my mother, Elvie Kidd, without whom I couldn't have become the woman I am today. To my son, Timothy Kidd, who is the reason I strive to be my best and who encourages me no matter what and loves me unconditionally. To my pastor, Bishop S. O. Bulloch Jr., a true prophet of God. He has been my spiritual leader for the past fifteen years and has taught me and helped me grow to be a strong servant of God.

Introduction

Where do I begin? While I was sitting at my computer one evening doing some homework, the Lord spoke to me. He said, "All is not lost."

I said, "Okay, Lord, but what do you mean?"

His voice was quiet, clear, and concise. He said, "That is the name of the book you will write."

Of course, I was baffled, because I had no idea what to do. So I prayed and kept asking him, "How am I supposed to do this, and what do I say."

He told me, "This book will help a vast amount of people, but I need you to be transparent and tell your story." Of course, I became afraid because of what I thought people would think about me; but he reassured my spirit and reminded me that it didn't matter what people would think about me, because I would be doing his will; and the only person I needed to be concerned about was my Heavenly Father. "So to you, Lord, I will be obedient and be transparent. And in doing your will, I pray that I can help someone who has experienced some of the things that I have and show them that with Christ, all things are possible."

> *"Before I formed you in the womb I knew you, and before you were born I consecrated you, I appointed you a prophet to the nations"* (Jer. 1:5, KJV).

I had no idea how true that statement would be concerning my life. Let me introduce myself. My name is Tanya. You may ask the question, just who is Tanya? I have asked myself that same question multiple times. Well, let me tell you just who I am. First and foremost, I am the child of the Almighty God Jehovah. I am the daughter of Arthur Kidd Sr. and Elvie Kidd. My parents loved me unconditionally, my mother is a godly woman who keeps me grounded. I am the mother of a blessed and highly favored son of God by the name of Timothy Kidd, I am a baby sister to three sisters and one brother by the name of Arthur Kidd Jr., I am an aunt, a cousin, niece, a friend to some, and perceived enemy to others.

So you see, I am just like any one of you. The only difference between me and other people at this point in my life is the fact that I have accepted and embraced my assignment from God Almighty. Don't misunderstand by no means, I fought this revelation for years. One thing I have learned is that when God has called you to do his work, no matter how much you try to run or fight against it, you will lose.

My assignment from the moment I was formed in my mother's womb has been to provide comfort, direction, and counsel, and to usher in healing to the body, mind, and spirit of the individuals that I encounter. This revelation knowledge was confirmed to me by my pastor, Bishop S. O. Bulloch of Grace Full Gospel Church in Savannah, Georgia, during one of his 2013 sermons entitled, "You Can't Succeed Alone: You Need 5 Types of Relationships." In this sermon, one of the relationships he spoke about was the golden connections. Bishop Bulloch summarized four facts about golden connections that really stuck with me to this day. Golden connections are divine bridges that enable you to exit out of one season of blessing and go into the next. Golden connections are brief encounters in your life that can be a golden link. A golden connection should never be treated lightly. Lastly, God will move you from the pit into the palace throughout the days of your golden assignment. So every encounter I have with an individual now, I embrace it as a golden connection.

I am a clinical nurse specialist by profession but not by happenstance. I now know I was called by God to be a nurse. I have a passion to help others that I can't explain. It is this passion that has caused me great grief and great joy at the same time. A nurse is a servant to the people they encounter, with the purpose of providing comfort and to help alleviate pain. As a child of God, we are expected to be servants for Christ.

> *Servants, obey in all things your masters according to the flesh; not with eye service, as men pleasers; but in singleness of the heart, fearing God. And whatsoever ye do, do it heartily, as to the lord, and not unto men; knowing that of the Lord ye shall receive he reward of the inheritance: for ye serve the Lord Christ* (Col. 3:22–24, KJV).

1

The Battle Begins

June 29, 1969, was the day I was expected to be born; but the devil decided to launch the first of many attack plans to kill me. My mother was in labor and in great pain. When she was admitted into the hospital and was checked, they found I was a breech. The doctors turned me and informed my mother's primary OB/GYN to deliver me because I was full term; and if they didn't perform the C-section, I would turn back and cause more problems. My mother's doctor told her that he didn't want to perform a C-section because my father was in Vietnam and there would not be anyone to help her take care of the newborn baby. This was a major problem because my mother's OB/GYN was the chief at the hospital, and no one could overturn his orders. My mother went back home in pain.

On July 30, 1969, my mother was rushed back to the hospital paralyzed with pain. She was found to have low blood count and had to wait for the blood to be delivered from another hospital. It was during this time that her physician received a call that his wife was ill, so he had to leave. Once the blood arrived, a team consisting of four physicians rushed my mother to surgery and performed a C-section because I had indeed turned back to breech.

After the procedure, they discovered that my first layer of skin had totally been eaten away. Since my mother carried me an extra thirty days, the amniotic fluid had become acidic to my skin and caused it all to slough off. I was rushed to a sterile tent, where I was placed on a ventilator. My mother, at that point, had become septic. My father was just returning from his deployment in Vietnam and was rushed to the hospital just in time for the doctors and the priest to inform him that my mother was gravely ill, and that if I made it through the night, I would have a 50/50 chance of survival past one week.

Needless to say, the devil's first attack failed. I was a fighter from day one, because God had a plan for my life that the devil couldn't stop. I stayed in the sterile tent for two weeks before they released me to travel with my parents to Savannah, Georgia. My father had new orders to go back to Vietnam, but during this traumatic time in my life, my grandfather passed, and my father had to make the trip to Mississippi alone to bury his father, come back and see me in the hospital at Hunter Army Airfield before boarding a plane back to Vietnam. I often wonder how my father dealt with everything.

I would later find out that everything is not always as it appears.

By the time I was three years old, the doctors realized that because I lost the first layer of my skin at birth, I had also lost my first line of immunity. During this time, I was sent to a specialist, who performed a variety of tests on me. It was determined that I was allergic to the environment—insects, animals, and the air. Thank the Lord I wasn't allergic to food. My parents were now faced with having to make life changes for me. My parents were told that in order for me to survive, I would have to have injections at least three times a week for the rest of my life, to boost my immunity. I would also have to carry an epinephrine pen for emergency purposes, just in case I was bitten by any ants, bees, or wasps. So I went to the military clinic every Monday, Wednesday, and Friday for my injections. These would continue until I turned eighteen. The devil's plan failed again. I didn't know then, but the calling was on my life; and no matter what the devil had planned, God had the bigger and better plan for me.

2

The Foundation Is Laid

"Train up a child in the way he should go, and when he is old he will not depart from it" (Prov. 22:6, KJV).

I have read that scripture more times than I can remember, and I will agree that it is true. I can't remember a time that I was not in church. I was raised by a saved and sanctified mother. And though my father was not saved, he supported my mother and the fact that she was a Christian. I was raised Pentecostal Holiness. As far back as I can remember, every Monday night, we had prayer service; Wednesday nights were Bible study; and Friday nights were regular testimony service. Not to mention, of course, Sunday school and regular church on Sunday morning and Sunday night. Going to church was not an option in our house; when it was time to go, we went. My father would fuss at me and my brother if we took too much time getting ready for church. It didn't matter if we had homework or chores; we went to church and finished whatever we needed to do when we returned home.

When we were not in church, we had Bible study at home. We read the Bible everyday as children, and I truly believe that because my mother was so insistent on teaching us about the Lord our God, I had something to hold on to in my later years. We even played Bible games as a family. As I recall this time in my life, it brings back so many wonderful memories.

During the summer when everyone else was hanging out and going on vacations, were went to vacation Bible school. I remember being excited to attend every summer because I learned so many new things every year. There were so many activities presented to us that I never wanted it to end. I was always a very inquisitive child, constantly asking questions to anyone that would listen. Learning about God was so fascinating to me that I just wanted to know more.

Children are pure, innocent, submissive, and trusting. This is the reason Christ said, "*Verily I say unto you, except ye be converted, and become as little children, ye shall not enter into the kingdom of heaven*" (Matt. 18:3, KJV). It is during our childhood that we are most receptive to information and develop our beliefs. This was the time in my life that I was drawn so close to God it didn't matter to me what people thought about me or what they believed. I was happy knowing I was a child of God. I was baptized at the age of ten and received Christ at age of twelve. I remember how much I enjoyed going to church and serving God. I became a youth leader, I sang in the choir, I represented my church at conventions. My childhood was filled with church, church activities, reading, and seeking more knowledge about Jesus Christ. This foundation would be my salvation.

Being the daughter of a military soldier had its good times and bad times. I was usually alone, in the sense that I had few friends because we moved so frequently. You might say, "Well, I had my siblings to keep me company." Well, yes, I had my brother who was four years older than me. My sisters were fifteen years older than me. During this time, my sisters didn't travel with my parents; they stayed with their grandparents because they wanted more stabilization in their lives, and also because they were almost adults themselves. So it was just my brother and me who traveled with our parents. The funny thing about that situation was the fact that my loving brother (haha) didn't like having a baby sister around because he thought I had taken his place; and every chance he had, he tried to give me away to whoever came to our house. For a child, this was hurtful experience. I know now, though, that he wasn't trying to be evil.

By the time I was in middle school, I began to make friends, but was frequently teased because I was the little saved girl that couldn't wear pants, only dresses. Children can be so cruel when they don't understand something. I survived the ridicule and kept my faith in God. As far back as I can remember, I have always been the type of person to keep to myself. In school, I was considered the little nerd, always at home reading a book or listening to music.

One day I decided to go outside and watch the guys in my neighborhood play football. I remember I was twelve years old, and I saw for the first time a young man, whom I developed a crush on. This was my first time having feelings for the opposite sex. I thought he was the cutest guy I had ever seen. He came to my house one evening and asked my mother if he could talk to me. My mom quickly rebuked him and told him I was twelve, he was sixteen. Needless to say, he was shocked, and my mom told him that I wasn't allowed to talk to boys and that we could only be friends. So we became best friends. Who would have ever thought we would be best friends to this very day through thick and thin. I didn't.

By the time I reached high school, I was ready to come out of my shell, sort of; speak; and make new friends. I was very happy with my high school and being a Wolverine. I was excelling in my classes and voted most likely to succeed by my senior class. I later became a cheerleader and was nominated by my senior class to run for Homecoming Queen. I didn't win. I did develop some lasting friendships, and I was on my way to college and looking forward to a bright, successful future. My life was good. But then something happened that would change the course of my life forever.

3

Innocence Lost

It was a Friday night, and we had a pep rally at school. I, as usual, would not have attended; but I wanted to spend some time with my friends. I rode with my brother, who was a senior at that time, to the pep rally. The rally was awesome, and I had a really great time with my friends. After the rally, I was unable to find my brother so we could go home.

After I had searched for about thirty minutes, a guy I knew from the swimming pool I attended for swimming lessons saw me and said he would take me home. I didn't see anything wrong with it, because I knew him—or so I thought. He was a senior like my brother, but he attended a different high school. The only thing I can say now is, people, trust your gut feeling. It's usually correct 99.9 percent of the time. I got into his car, and halfway from my house, he said he had to pick up his cousin from his house. I said okay, not thinking at all. My inexperience with boys had me at a place where I trusted what they said to me. We picked up his cousin, and as we left, he took a detour into a long, dark road that led to a wooded area.

That's when I knew I was in trouble. But it was too late. We didn't have cell phones then, so I was at their mercy. No one could hear me out there. I tried to get out of the car and run, but they both grabbed me, and one held me down while the other raped me; and then the other held me down while the other one raped me. They took turns for what felt like an eternity. I was crying, kicking, and screaming; but they covered my mouth. I thought I was about to suffocate under their weight. When they were done with me, they drove me to the foot of the bridge that led to my house and let me out of the car and drove away.

As I walked up and over the bridge in the dark, all I could think about was the pain I was feeling. And then what was my mother going to say about my new dress that was now torn and stained with my blood?. I couldn't believe what had just happened to me. I was a virgin, and I couldn't believe that was how I lost my virginity. I felt so sick and stupid for trusting him.

I finally reached my house and quickly realized that my mom and my dad were both asleep. I guess they were resting because I was with my brother, and they didn't have any reason to worry. Little did they know how wrong that assumption would be. I ran to my room, took off the dress, and put it in a trash bag. I got in the shower and cried as I watched the water stained with my blood going down the drain. I felt the essence of me going down the drain with the blood. I scrubbed and scrubbed until I felt raw, but I couldn't seem to get the scent of them off of me.

Finally, I gave up and got out of the shower went to my room and sat on my bed and cried. I heard my brother come in, and I put a pillow over my face to mask my crying. He didn't come into my room; he just opened the door. I guess he wanted to be sure I was home. He closed the door, and I cried until I had no more tears left. I tried to sleep but kept waking up; all I could see were their faces, and I couldn't stop hearing their voices. I was in so much pain I didn't know what to do. This was the longest night I had ever experienced in my life. The night my life changed forever.

I never told my parents, my best friend, or my brother what happened to me that night. I did tell one person—a good friend of mine in my homeroom class. We talked, and she told me I had to get tested for STDs and to make sure I wasn't pregnant. I thought, *Oh God, I can't be pregnant.* I felt at that moment that I could just die.

I went to the health department and got tested, but was informed I had to wait two weeks for the results. Those were the longest, most agonizing two weeks of my life. Thank the Lord Almighty everything came back negative. I felt some relief, but I was still having nightmares and being haunted about that night. I never spoke of the rape again until years later when I told my mom and my best friend. I didn't seek any counseling or talk about it. I buried all the pain and shame in my subconscious. Or so I thought.

4

Hopelessness

After the rape, I questioned my faith in God. I wanted to know why he allowed that to happen to me. Why didn't he protect me? Well, I didn't blame God. I just thought that no matter where I was or what I was doing, he would always protect me from harm. What I didn't know then was that God was in control even at that very moment. The disciple James explains it best: *"My brethren, count it all joy when you fall into various trials. Knowing that the testing of your faith produces patience. But let patience have its perfect work, that you may be perfect* and *complete lacking nothing"* (James 1:2–3, NIV).

During this time in my life, I had become very good at hiding my emotions and putting on a happy face, all the while dying inside. As close as I was to my best friend, Tony, I never confided in him what was going on with me. He was four years my senior, and he had become my protector; but I still felt I couldn't tell him everything. Even though we talked on a daily basis, I wanted to open up to him because I had no one else; but the pain and the shame was too deep.

I managed to make it through high school and was ready to start college. My brother introduced me to a young man who would later become my first boyfriend. I thought he would be my future husband, but that would not be the case, because he married someone else. He moved away, and I moved back home with my parents. I thought, *Another failure to add to my life.*

One Monday afternoon, I was lying on my bed when my mother came to my room and began screaming at me. I jumped up and asked her what was wrong. She pulled me off the bed and pushed me in front of the mirror, and I couldn't believe my eyes. I was so swollen from my face, arms, and legs; I looked bloated. She rushed me to the hospital, and they performed all sorts of test. They performed a urine pregnancy test, and it was negative, so I felt relieved; but then they did a blood test that revealed I was, indeed, pregnant and had a condition called preeclampsia. They performed an ultrasound that revealed I was measuring six and a half months pregnant.

I was more than shocked. I had no symptoms, and I had a regular cycle each month. I was so confused and hurt and alone. My mom was fussing over me, saying I had no prenatal care, and that anything could be wrong with the baby. I was terrified by this time. My life as I knew it was over. Thinking back now I did not recall feeling my baby move. I felt my future slipping away from me. Little did I know that God had my life already planned for me, and it included my unborn child.

5

Determination

The hardest thing I had to do was tell my father that I was pregnant. I didn't want to disappoint him like that. His baby girl—single and pregnant. Well, I did; and he was surprised but was very supportive. At that moment, I knew everything would be all right, because my father forgave me and he loved me.

I continued going to college, never missing a day of class. My father attended my prenatal appointments with me, and my life was good. Or so I thought. The devil had other plans, as usual. The rest of my pregnancy was a little rough. I was diagnosed with preeclampsia and prediabetes. I gained over sixty pounds and was miserable.

On April 7, 1989, I went into labor. My mom was at my side, but after twelve hours of labor, the doctor came and told me I could go home because my labor had stopped. But I refused to go home. Shifts changed, and the new doctor assessed me and said I needed a little help with my delivery. They placed an electric monitor on my abdomen to induce the contractions. Unfortunately, they induced me more than they had anticipated.

On April 8, 1989, at 6:30 p.m., I started having difficulty breathing. The baby's heartbeat dropped rapidly. I was immediately taken to the delivery room, where I was told to push. I was on 4 liters of oxygen and in excruciating pain. I was in a military hospital, where they did not practice giving epidurals or providing any type of pain medication during delivery. So I had to go through natural childbirth while having breathing difficulties. After three attempts to push, the physicians yelled to me to stop pushing because the baby's head was out but the umbilical cord was wrapped around his neck twice. The baby couldn't breathe, and neither could I. The doctor told me not to move. Well, that was a problem, seeing that the baby was halfway out and I was in so much pain. But then he said I could break the baby's neck, so I froze. They removed the cord, and I gave birth to a beautiful baby boy. The devil had indeed tried to take us both out, but God had other plans.

I was finally happy for a change. All I could think about was how I wanted to make a wonderful life for my son. I went back to college after three days, because I was in nursing school, and I was determined to finish on time. My father became my biggest support. He was my baby sitter while I attended classes. I did receive government assistance, but I decided I would do whatever it took to succeed, so I started working three part-time jobs while going to school, and I was able to get off government assistance. I wanted the best for my son, and I was determined to sacrifice everything to provide a successful future for him. He was the only important thing in my life, and I wanted to make him proud one day. I made a vow to God that I was going to put my son's well-being first, with his guidance.

6

My Faith Tested

After the birth of my son, I thought I had my life under control. My faith in God had been restored, and I was doing well in college. I started dating, but all the men I dated wanted only one thing, and that wasn't what I wanted.

On April 15, 1991, I met a young man who was in the military and we started dating. Life was good for me, but soon my life would take another blow that would bring me back to my knees. We had been dating for about five months when on September 16, 1991, I received the worst news I could imagine.

I was home with my father and my son that day, and my father, who was already partially paralyzed from an incident while he was in the military during the Vietnam War, all of a sudden kept falling down. I would help him up, but after the third fall, I called EMS. Earlier that morning, I had taken my mother to the military hospital in Hinesville to have surgery on her eyes. They said that it would be an extensive surgery, so I came home to check on my father and my son.

The EMS took my father to the same hospital that my mother was having her surgery, I followed in my car. I was there with my son, and I felt all alone. My brother was now in the air force, stationed at Pope Air Force Base, in North Carolina, so of course, he couldn't help me at that time. I prayed, and the young man that I had been dating was stationed at Fort Stewart where the hospital was located. I called his commander and asked, could he come be by my side since I now had both parents in the hospital and a two-year-old son. His commander sent him over to the hospital to be with me just as the doctor came into the room to talk to me.

There were four doctors in the room, and I could tell the news I was about to receive would not be good. The doctors began to explain to me that my father had metastatic brain cancer, with three tumors the size of grapefruits (as they described them), and that they wanted to perform surgery immediately and then send him to Dwight Eisenhower Army Hospital. I just froze. I couldn't wrap my mind around what they were telling me. I thought, *No, not my daddy. Not my rock, my provider, my father, my friend, not the first man I ever loved that loved me back unconditionally. Not him.* I told the doctors I couldn't make that decision because my mom was upstairs as we spoke, having her eyes operated on. I just couldn't do anything at that point.

Just then, my father looked at me and said, "I want to see you get married before I die."

I thought, *Daddy, that's the last thing on my mind.*

He continued, "Tanya, you are a beautiful young woman inside and out, and I want to make sure you finish college, get married so that I can be at peace knowing you have someone looking out for you and my grandson because you are my baby, and you deserve to have it all."

I just stood there in shock; and then all of a sudden, the young man I had been dating for only five months asked me to marry him right there in front of my dad. I was so confused. But then I thought if I say yes, it would give him peace, so I said yes.

Four hours had passed, and the EMS came to transport my father to the hospital in Augusta, Georgia. I'd never seen my father cry. He was a Vietnam War veteran, and he had gone through a lot during the war; but there he was, looking up at me with tears running down his face. He said, "You will soon forget all about me." I cried and said, "Never, Daddy. I will call you as soon as you get to the hospital and have settled in your room." Little did I know that the hospital he was going to didn't have phones in the patients' rooms. My life had now taken another blow that shook me to my core.

They moved my mom into the recovery area. There I stood over her bed with tears in my eyes, terrified to tell her that the man she had loved and been married to for over thirty years had just been diagnosed with metastatic brain cancer and was taken to the Army Hospital in Augusta. I cried so hard and said to myself, *Where are you, God? Why are you allowing this to happen to me?* My faith in God was tested again. Right then I remembered a Bible verse I learned: *"Have I not commanded you? Be strong and courageous? Do not be afraid, do not be discouraged in the Lord you God will be with you wherever you go"* (Josh. 1:9, KJV). After that, I was able to tell my mom the news; and to my surprise, she was calm and said God was in control.

7

Taking Charge of My Life

After we left the hospital and got home, I immediately called the hospital where my father had been taken and asked to speak to him. The nurse informed me that there we no phones in the rooms, but she would relay a message. I screamed at her at the top of my lungs, telling her that they better find a phone because I promised my father I would call, and he could hear our voices so he wouldn't feel that we had forgotten about him. I then told the nurse that if she didn't find one as soon as possible, I would drive up there immediately in the middle of the night if I had to. The nurse found an extension cord and was able to give the phone to my father. It felt so good hearing his voice, and I could tell he was happy to hear mine, and that I kept my promise to him. I told him we would be there over the weekend to see him. I then gave the phone to my mother, and they talked for a while.

The young man I had been dating took the engagement seriously. he went and bought me a ring and asked me to marry him, again. I was so overwhelmed that all I could think about was how happy that would make my father. Don't get me wrong, I cared for my boyfriend deeply, but I was thinking we would have a long engagement, at least a year, so that we could get to know each other better. That wasn't going to happen, because my father had less than six months to give.

We were married on September 21, 1991, in a private ceremony at my church surrounded by my family. It was a beautiful ceremony, and I was a happy bride. After the ceremony, everyone got into their cars, still dressed in their wedding attire, and we drove to the hospital in Augusta where my father was, just to surprise him. The look on my father's face was priceless. He finally got his wish—his baby girl was married, and there we all were, his family, surrounding him at his bedside. Everyone was so happy and the staff was so encouraging and gave us a small wedding party while we were there. Just as we were about to leave, the doctors came in to the room to talk to my mother. They told her that my father needed to be transferred to a hospice because there was nothing more they could do for him. My mother told the doctors to order the move to the hospice and any equipment that we would need to bring him home.

The doctors informed my mom that she didn't understand what she was going to be dealing with by taking him home. My mother told them that my father wanted to come home, and she was going to do everything in her power to make that happen. The doctors then ordered a hospital bed, a bedside commode, a wheel-chair, and a Hoyer lift to be sent to our house because my father was coming home. My brother put in for a humanitarian transfer to a base closer to home.

8

Shattered Dreams

My father came home in October of 1991, and my mother, my aunts, and I took care of him. I was a junior in college majoring in nursing. The one thing I remember the most during this time was the fact that at no time did my father scream or cry or holler out in pain. The cancer had spread from his lungs to his brain and now to his bones. I knew he was in pain, but not once did he show it. My mother had to make him take the morphine because she knew he was in excruciating pain. My father was a very strong man in every way. He spent his days talking to mom and holding the only grandchild he would ever know. My brother was married but didn't have any children at that time; he would come home on the weekends to see my father.

I remember the doctors telling my mom the tumors in Dad's brain could rupture at any time. One Friday morning, I was up getting ready for work and I went into the room where my father was sleeping. I was met with the sight of an abundance of a black substance over the wall and over my father. My first thought was that the tumors had indeed ruptured and my father was dead. I quickly closed the door, because I didn't want my mother to see my father this way. I approached the bed. He was so quiet, and then all of a sudden, he coughed, and more of the black substance came out. I then realized that the black substance was not the remnant of the tumors—it was emesis, which occurred while it was coming out of his stomach to be coughed out, causing it to spread all over like it did.

I was so relieved, I quickly cleaned him up before my mother woke up. My father was 6'1" tall and usually weighed 190 pounds, but there he was now, only about 110 pounds. The cancer had completely taken over his entire body, and he was now so frail. I prayed daily for my father to have peace from all the pain. Watching him get smaller and smaller day after day was breaking my heart. I couldn't understand how my mother kept it together. She never cried in front of us or my dad. She just faithfully took care of the man she had loved all her adult life.

On November 23, 1991, at approximately 5:00 p.m., I received a call from my mom while I was at work. She told me that my father's fever broke and that he was feeling much better. I was working over-time that day, and suddenly, I felt a crushing pain in my chest. I felt that I needed to go home. My supervisor told me I had to stay. I told her that they had plenty of help, and I needed to go home right then.

I called my husband to come get me, and I asked him how my father was doing. He informed me that when he left the house, my dad was talking to my mom and my aunt and was in a good mood laughing with them all. He was watching my son play next to his bed. I told him okay, but I had a bad feeling that I couldn't shake.

When I opened the front door and walked in, I saw everyone sitting in the living room crying, all except my mom. I looked at my mom, and she said so calmly, "I'm sorry, baby, but he's gone." I ran to his room, and there he was, lying there looking so peaceful as if he was just sleeping; but when I touched him, he was ice cold. I couldn't believe he was gone and I didn't get a chance to say good-bye or tell him how much I loved and still needed him. I was so angry that I left his room and punched a hole in the hall wall and then fell to my knees and cried. My father, my dad was now gone. He left us the day before Thanksgiving. My brother's orders had just been approved when my mom called him. He came straight to the house, then he went to process in at Charleston Air Force. The only thing I knew was that Thanksgiving would never be the same for me.

9

Depression Takes Over

We didn't celebrate Thanksgiving the next day because no one was in the mood to cook or really socialize. We were all still numb from losing my father. I remember praying and asking questions that we all do. Why did God take my dad? Didn't he know how much I needed him? If there's one thing I have learned in my walk with God, it's to never question God. He will sometimes answer you, and sometimes he won't, but he will always be in charge. I couldn't blame God, so I became bitter and angry with everyone that tried to comfort me. To make matters worse, I was now married, and I didn't know how to be a wife at all, so I did what was familiar to me and shut down, keeping all my hurt inside.

After my father's funeral, my life went downhill. I was married to a man I really didn't know, trying to be a wife, to finish college, and to raise my son. Nothing was going as planned. My husband started having an affair with his coworker and using drugs. At first it was cocaine. Then he went on to using crack, and then meth. To cope with everything, I started gambling. In the beginning, I won more than I lost; but everything eventually evens out, and I began to lose more than I won.

I thought the joy of winning would fill the emptiness I had in my heart, but it just made things worse, and I felt more alone than before. You may ask, "Why didn't you turn to God?" Well, the trick of the devil is to make you feel so ashamed of what you are doing at the time that you believe that God doesn't love you and you become paralyzed and afraid to seek God.

I began to hate my life even more; I was so miserable. On May 5, 2000, decided I wanted to stop all my pain and end my life. I took the pills out, laid them under my pillow, and took a shower. All I can say is, but God!

After taking my shower, I got dressed to go to church with my family. Knowing all along what I had planned to do when I got home. It was all planned out—that is, until I got to church that Sunday and my bishop read the scripture from Jeremiah 29:11 (NIV): *"For I know plans that I have for you, declares the Lord, plans to prosper you and not to harm you, plans to give you hope and a future."* I was sitting in church and in the middle of his sermon, my pastor, Bishop S. O. Bulloch, stopped preaching and called me up to the front of the church. I know I hadn't done anything or told anyone about my plans for that day, so needless to say, I was very surprised when he called me up to the altar. He said to me, "The plans you have for later today, God said no, it will not happen." I literally froze. He proceeded to call my family up to the altar and told them to hug me because they didn't know how close they came to losing me that day. It was at that moment that I knew God had great plans for my life and he truly loved me.

10

Confusion

Over the next five years, I struggled to keep my marriage together; but it seemed the harder I tried, the worse it got. Getting married as quickly as I did, made it impossible for me to know the man I pledged to spend the rest of my life with. Unfortunately, I didn't know that my husband at the time had a serious drug problem.

After my father's death, I tried to lean on my husband for support; but little by little, I found out he was into cocaine. At first, I was furious—not with him so much as with myself. You see, I didn't seek God's guidance on marriage, so this was all my doing. Because I didn't seek God, I turned to gambling to try to cope.

I had just purchased my very own house, and I was happy. There were nights when my husband would leave in my car and wouldn't come home for days. There were so many times that I woke up to get ready for work just to find my car was not there and then have to walk to and from work after a twelve-hour shift because he had taken all the money I had.

One day, after working a twelve-hour shift, I called my husband to tell him I was ready to be picked up. He told me he was on his way. After waiting for over an hour, I began walking home. As I began walking, I noticed my car coming toward me with my husband in it and a woman that I didn't know. He drove right past me and, apparently, took her home. He came back to where he saw me, and I was still standing there in disbelief. I was past furious; I told him to get out of my car and give me my keys because I'd had enough, and we were done. He started laughing at me, which made me even more furious. As he got out of the car, he threw my keys over to the grass. I was so angry I forgot I had a can of Coke in my hand and I threw it at him, hitting him in the heard. Just as that happened, a policeman was driving by and saw what I did. At this time, my husband was bleeding from the laceration on his head. The officer approached us both and said that he had witnessed the whole thing; but in fact, he didn't. He only saw what I did.

The officer asked my husband, was he okay; and of course, he said no and played the victim. I tried to explain to the officer what really happened, but the officer didn't want to hear what I had to say. He proceeded to place me under arrest for simple battery. I couldn't believe this was happening. Here I was, going to jail while he had my car, my house, and access to everything I owned. He just stood there smiling while we drove off.

There I was, going to jail for simple battery. I thought, *God, where are you now? Why is it that I'm the one going to jail and not him?* I couldn't understand any of it. I remember my mother would always say that God doesn't put more on you than you can bear. That didn't even make sense to me at that time.

I was processed, and then I called a friend of mine named Pamela. She came and got one of my debit cards to pay my bail. All I could think about was going home and getting some rest before work the next day. I called to see where my husband was; but of course, he didn't answer the phone. I was released and started walking home because I had used all my money to pay my bond. My friend had gone back to work, so there I was, stuck again.

It was 1:30 a.m., when I finally reached my home; and to my surprise, my husband was there, asleep in bed. I was tired and didn't want to deal with him, so I went to the guestroom and got ready to go to bed. I guess I was making too much noise because he woke up.

He came to the room and said he was calling the police to take me back to jail because he was the victim and he was in fear for his life.

The police arrived, and he proceeded to tell him what had transpired the previous day and that I wasn't supposed to be anywhere near him due to him being afraid of me and the assault that occurred. The officer asked if it was true and I proceeded to tell him yes and that I had just gotten home from being in jail. I was silently praying to the Lord; and all of a sudden, the officer asked whose house it was, and we both stated that it was my house. So the officer informed my husband that due to the fact that it was my house and he was feeling that he would be in danger with me there, he had to leave and find somewhere else to stay until we went to court. My husband looked stunned, but I was thanking God. The officer waited until he left. God had worked it out for me.

I was able to sleep in my bed peacefully that night. Then the hospital called and said they had too many nurses on the schedule and that I could take the day off. I replied, "No problem." My God came through for me again and allowed me to have some time to myself and be at peace for the next few days. Although we had our bad times, I still wanted my marriage to work. I didn't want to get a divorce because I took my vows very seriously. At this time, my self-esteem was very low, and I found myself on many occasions trying to do anything to keep my husband.

One day, I decided to surprise him and take him to lunch so we could sit and talk. I went to the back section where he worked, and to my surprise, I saw him kissing his coworker. I couldn't believe my eyes, so I started screaming at both of them. I ran out of the building to get in my car and leave. As I was walking across the parking lot, I heard a car coming. I turned around and saw it was the woman he was kissing, and she was headed straight toward me. My mind told me to jump, and I did. I landed on the hood of her car. She then made a sharp turn to throw me off. I landed on the pavement, but she kept driving. Just then, an old classmate of mine happened to see the whole thing and came to my side. He called an ambulance and stayed with me until they came. I remember falling asleep, but they kept trying to wake me up. I kept saying, "My head hurts," and the doctor told me I had landed on my head and had a big laceration on it.

The devil tried to take me out again, but God had a different plan. God sent an angel to watch over me and be at my side until I was taken to the hospital. I was very appreciative but also very sad because my husband was not by my side. This would be one of many affairs that my husband would have during our marriage. I thought it was my fault that he was cheating and treating me the way that he did. For everyone reading this book, it's not your fault. They have the problem. They want you to believe you are the reason they have to cheat on you. That is just one of the many tricks of the devil to keep you from believing in and trusting God.

11

Lost

I was still married to my husband, and we both were ordered to go to counseling—me for anger management and him for drug addiction. I really never stopped to think about how I dealt with my anger before going to the mandatory counseling. Needless to say, I never handled my anger in a positive way. I usually kept things bottled up inside so I didn't have to deal with anything. I would go and gamble to take my mind off of what was going on in my life. Of course, the only thing that did was make things worse.

Here I was, married and stressed, to the point that my beautiful hair was falling out, all because I married a man I didn't know had a drug problem, and because I didn't deal with my own problems. He would take the food from the house and sell it on the streets. Then I would spend my hard-earned money and extra time gambling. We were on a collision course, and neither of us could see it. The problem was that I didn't seek God for help in this situation, or on a constant basis. God will not push his way into our livers; he must be invited in. If you seek him, he will be there. He says in Jeremiah 29:13 (KJV), *"You will seek me and find me, when you seek me with all your heart."*

The problem I had was the fact that I knew the way of the Lord, but I still didn't trust him or seek him with my whole heart. I thought I had everything under control; undoubtedly, I was very wrong. I let the devil trick me again.

On July 30, 2010, it all came to an end. I walked into our bedroom and told to my husband that I was willing to give my marriage one last chance, but he had to meet me halfway. I informed him that when I came home from work, we would go out and have dinner, celebrate my birthday, and talk about the problems in our marriage. I went on to tell him that if I came home and he was high, that it would be the end of our marriage and I would file for divorce. We had been married for nineteen years, and I wanted to make it work. I remember my pastor at that time told me I had to make my marriage work. There was no other option according to God.

Well, I came home from work, and what did I find? Yes, you guessed it. My husband was so high he was oblivious to the fact that I was standing there. At the very moment, I told my husband I was no longer his wife, and I moved all my things into my guestroom. The next day, I filed for divorce. Don't get me wrong, I stuck by him for nineteen years and three episodes of in-house rehab. He just didn't want to stop. I had to think about my life and the example I was setting for my son. I had to get help for myself.

I tried to get him to go to counseling with me, but he refused. My divorce was very difficult. I had various people telling me that if I went through with my divorce, I would be committing adultery and I would never be able to marry again. I'm so thankful to my bishop and his wisdom. I went to him and asked him what could I do as a Christian and not be doomed to go to hell for adultery. As always, my bishop gave me the Word of God. You must read the Bible for yourself, and then you will know what the Lord says about any circumstance.

He reminded me to read Matthew 19:9 (KJV). *"And I say unto you, whosoever shall put away his wife except it be for fornication, and shall marry another woman, committed adultery: and whosoever marrieth her which is put away doth commit adultery."*

I thought, *Lord I'm doomed.*

But then he gave me the other part of God's Word from 1 Corinthians 7:11–15 (KJV):

But if she does, she must remain unmarried or else be reconciled with her husband. And a husband must not divorce his wife. To the rest I say this, if any brother has a wife who is not a believer and she is willing to live with him, he must not divorce her. And if a woman has a husband who is not a believer and he is willing to live with her, she must not divorce him. For the unbelieving husband is sanctified by the wife, and the unbelieving wife is sanctified by the husband: else were your children unclean but now they are holy. But if the unbeliever depart, let him depart. A brother or sister is not under bondage in such cases: but God has called us to peace.

After I had prayed and fasted, the Lord revealed to me that since my husband was not a believer, he was free to go and I was free to remarry—but only to another believer, and he must be saved. No longer could I be unequally yoked. My husband finally moved out of the house at the thirty-day deadline that the court put in place. I wasn't home at the time; I was at Fort Valley University picking up my son for spring break. I called my mom to ask if he was gone yet. She said he was. At that moment, I was happy and sad at the same time.

When we reached home, my son ran to the bedroom just to see if he was, in fact, gone. He yelled out at me, "Mom, you don't want to see this."

I went to the bedroom, and I was met with a shocking reality. My soon-to-be ex-husband had taken everything out of our room, leaving only the mattress; and in the corner, he had taken all my clothes and cut them to shreds. All I could do was laugh and cry. My son thought I had lost my mind. I felt so relieved and happy because I could replace everything he had taken and destroyed, because now I had my peace of mind back. I was so elated I started to fall back onto the mattress until I heard a soft voice say, "Stop."

I asked my son, was he talking to me? And he replied that he hadn't said a word. So I fell back onto the bed again; and again, I heard the voice telling me to stop. I looked at my son and said, "Let's pull up the mattress." To my surprise, my soon-to-be ex-husband had taken all the cushion out of the mattress, and fifteen knives were strategically placed inside the mattress and taped so they could stand up. Now I don't know if he did it on purpose or if he did it while he was high, because he was constantly paranoid.

Once again, the devil tried to take me out. If I didn't listen to the small voice of Christ whispering in my ear, I would have been stabbed to death. All I could do was cry out in praise, "Thank you, Jesus." God saved me again. If you take anything away from this book, remember this: Please, men and women, listen to that small voice within yourself that tells you right instead of wrong. It is truly the voice of the Lord."

Ezekiel 3:17–19 (KJV) reads,

> *Son of man, I have made you a watchman unto the house of Israel: therefore hear the word at my mouth, and give them warning from me. When I say unto the wicked, Thou shalt surely die; and thou givest him not warning, nor speakest to warn the wicked from the wicked way, to save his life; the same wicked way, to save his life: the same wicked man shall die in his iniquity; but by blood will I require at thine hand. Yet if thou warn the wicked, and he turn not from his wicked ways, he shall die in his iniquity: but thou hast delivered thy soul.*

God will allow us ample opportunities to change our ways and live for him. The unfortunate part of human nature is that we seek God when we are in trouble; but then when he delivers us, we go right back to our wicked ways. This is a daily struggle according to Ephesians 6:11 (KJV). *"Put on the whole armour of God, that ye may be able to stand against the wiles of the devil."*

12

Freedom

It took over eight months, but I was able to finally get my divorce. I had absolutely nothing to my name. Everything that I had in storage was taken and sold for God knows what. Here I was, forty-two and starting all over from scratch.

I had my health, and I had a job; but there was something missing in my life. My best friend and I were not on speaking terms, and that situation had me feeling depressed. But as I now look back on the time we spent apart not communicating, I realize that the five months we spent apart gave me some time to get to know myself and break some habits. But how many of you know that when you are at the point in your life that feels it is the lowest, that's when you become most vulnerable to the devil.

Things had gotten better between myself and my best friend. But as we all know, when things look good and you feel your life is on track, here comes the devil again. I was diagnosed with cervical cancer and fibroids. When I say I didn't see that coming, believe me, I didn't. The devil was once again trying to take my life.

I discussed my problem with my best friend, and like always, he was there for me. In March of 2012, I temporarily moved in with him. On March 29, 2012, he took me to the hospital to have my hysterectomy. Before we went, I had a terrible feeling that I should postpone the procedure. I should have listened to that quiet voice telling me not to go, but I didn't. I listened to everyone else instead of listening to that voice within me giving me warning.

My OB/GYN told me it would be a simple surgery and my downtime would only be two weeks maximum. Well, I trusted and believed him and had the procedure. My hospital stay was overnight, and I was released the next day, which was a Saturday. My best friend took me to his house to recover. Needless to say, that's when all my problems would surface and the devil decided to put another plan to kill me into action.

While I was at Tony's house, his family came over to provide some support. His sister noticed that my stomach was very distended and suggested I take some Epsom salt to help move my bowels. She gave me some in a cup, and I drank it. I took a total of three glasses of the Epsom salt water over the next two days. My abdomen remained distended, but I didn't have the urge neither did I have a bowel movements, not even any gas.

On the following Monday, which was April 1, 2012, Tony woke up and got ready for work. He asked if I needed any help going to the bathroom. I informed him that I still didn't have the urge to go, but that I would be okay. Around 10:00 a.m., I tried to get out of bed and was suddenly struck with a pain in my abdomen. I had never felt that kind of pain in my life, not even during childbirth. I fell to the floor and could not get up. I pulled the phone down and called Tony at work. He informed me to call an ambulance and he would meet me at the hospital. The pain was so agonizing. I quickly called my son instead of the ambulance. To this day, I don't know how my son got to me as fast as he did; but he was there in about ten minutes. He found me on the floor, picked me up, and placed me in the car and got me to the hospital in no time at all. While we were en route to the hospital, I called my OB/GYN who performed the surgery to inform him of the problem. He asked me to come to his office first. So I went to his office, which was right next to the hospital. He tried to examine my abdomen, but I was in so much pain that he told my son to take me to the admissions office in the hospital.

Ironically, this was the hospital where I had been employed as a registered nurse for the past ten years. So when I saw the team of colorectal physicians waiting for my in the admissions office, I knew it was serious. The chief surgeon informed me that they needed to take me to surgery because he was 99 percent sure I had a perforated bowel and an acute abdomen. I informed the surgery team that I needed them to confirm that with an abdominal scan, because I wasn't going into surgery on a guess. At that time, three of the surgeons placed me on a stretcher and took me to get a CT scan. Upon completion of the scan, I was immediately taken to surgery holding. I was informed that I had indeed suffered a perforated bowel during my recent hysterectomy. The chief surgeon also informed me that I may have to get a temporary colostomy. I signed the consent form to have the bowel resection, but I also wrote in solid-black ink, "NO COLOSTOMY."

I was taken into surgery at 11:00 a.m. on Monday, and I was wheeled in to the recovery room at 7:30 p.m. of that same Monday. The chief surgeon informed me that my bowel was severely perforated and he had to remove six inches of my colon and reconnect the severed sections, and also remove 50 percent of adhesions from my intestines. He informed my son that if he had not gotten me there when he did, I would have died from sepsis. The surgery took a long time because he had to clean out my abdomen because it was full of stool and bacteria caused by the hole made in my intestines by mistake.

The devil wasn't done yet. What was supposed to be a simple vaginal hysterectomy turned into the most complicated hospital stay of my life. While recovering from the second surgery, I suffered from numerous complications. My wound opened up due to an abscess, and I had to have another surgery to have that removed. I developed sepsis again, and two more abscesses, which required two more surgeries. I wasn't allowed to eat or drink anything; I wasn't passing any gas or stool. Every nourishment I received was by way of an IV. My weight dropped significantly from 170 pounds to 120 pounds. The initial surgery I had that should have been simple put me to be in the hospital for a total of four months. I had a total of four surgeries and was finally discharged with a wound vac to help expedite the healing process and skilled nursing at home.

Unfortunately, I managed to stay out of the hospital for only a week when I developed a fever of 103 degrees and was taken back. I was informed that I had another abscess. This time I prayed to God to intervene and help me. I know I should have been doing that all along. Well, like most people, I was scared and was not thinking rationally at this time. When I prayed this time, God heard me. I didn't have surgery; the physicians put me back in the hospital for a week of high-dose antibiotic therapy. Not only did God hear my prayer and step in for me, but to this day, I haven't had any issues with the part of my colon that was resected.

The devil wants us to be fearful; and despite knowing God is almighty, our flesh still reacts in fear. But God said in 2 Timothy 1:7 (KJV), *"For God has not given us the spirit of fear, but of power and of love and of a sound mind."* We as Christians must remember this at all times.

13

Torn

As much as I loved God, I had a major problem with my flesh. I wanted what I wanted when I wanted; and no matter how much God warned me or tried to guide me in his way, you guessed it, I disobeyed and tried to make things happen the way I wanted it to. Well, as you know, of course, my decisions only led to major heartbreak.

God doesn't want us to be alone according to his Word in Proverbs 18:22 (KJV): *"Whosoever findeth a wife findeth a good thing and obtain favor of the Lord."* The Bible does not have any scripture that says that a woman that findeth a husband findeth a good thing. The problem that I was facing was the fact that I was jealous, lonely, and impatient till I went looking for my mate instead of waiting for God to send him to me. We as women are even willing to share a man because the devil will have us listening to our emotions telling us that we will never have anyone, so we should settle for anything. If we have faith and keep trusting in God's Word, he will give us a mate that is good in his sight, and the union would be blessed by God instead of cursed and full of pain.

After the time I spent recovering, God was dealing with me to go in his direction, and my emotions were drawing me in another direction.

I was that woman. I was at what I thought was my lowest point in life. I just happened to run into an old classmate of mine. Ladies,

I have to admit, he was he everything I wanted in a man. He gave me so much attention, which was the main thing I had been missing in my marriage and in the relationship I now had with my best friend. He made me feel that I was the most important woman in the world. I wanted this young man for myself, and I did everything in my power to keep him.

This young man was so sweet to me; he made me feel beautiful and important to him. But how many of you know this: the devil knows what you need, and he will give you your hearts' desire— but at a cost. Since my previous relationships had failed miserably, I thought I was ready for a new one. I struggled within myself; but eventually, I gave in to my heart. The devil was using a different tactic this time to destroy me. I knew that God was telling me this was not my time yet, but I was so desperate just to keep him that I paid his bills and gave him money. He had complete access to me. I found out the hard way that he was involved with other women. But I didn't care at the time because I wanted to feel loved. I tried to force something that wasn't ordained by God, all because I was impatient and lonely. I don't blame him, or anyone for that matter, for what I went through. I put man above God.

Well, I learned something. God allowed me to go through all of this and experience all the pain I felt just to show me that I put my trust in man and that was the wrong thing to do. God was showing me that he loved me unconditionally from the beginning of my life, and by trusting in my own judgment, I would always make mistake after mistake. This was a learning experience for me. I had to go through this same cycle for three years before I finally decided to trust and listen to God.

One day, after crying for what I thought was hours, God spoke to my spirit and led me to read Jeremiah 29:11 (KJV). *"For I know the thoughts that I have toward you, saith the Lord, thoughts of peace and not of evil, to give you and expected end."* I was so anxious for a relationship in my life that I forgot what he said in 2 Corinthians 6:14-15 (KJV). *"Do not be yoked together with unbelievers. For what do righteousness and wickedness have in common? Or what fellowship can light have with darkness? What harmony is there between Christ and Belial? Or what part hath he that believeth with an infidel?"*

You would think I would have learned from being married to an unbeliever and not go down that same path. Well, I didn't. I let my flesh rule my heart. The main thing we as believers and women must remember about our desires and wants that we can't control is this Bible verse: *"For we wrestle not against flesh and blood, but against principalities, against powers, against the rulers of the darkness of the world, against spiritual wickedness in high places"* (Eph. 6:12, KJV).

Living for Christ is a daily battle against our flesh. As believers, we can't let our guard down at any time at all. Christ tells us this very thing in Ephesians 6:11, 6:12–18 (KJV).

> *Put on the whole armor of God that yea may be able to stand against the wiles of the devil. Wherefore take unto you the whole armor of God, that ye may be able to withstand in the evil day, and having done all, to stand. Stand, therefore, having your loins girt about with truth, and having on the breastplate of righteousness. And your feet shod with the preparation of the gospel of peace; above all, taking the shield of faith, where with ye shall be able to quench all the fiery darts of the wicked, and take the helmet of salvation, and the sword of the spirit, which is the word of God. Praying always with all prayer and in the spirit, and watching there unto with all perseverance and supplication for all saints.*

If we follow his Word, he will never lead us astray but will always keep us covered with his blood, provide us with his favor over our lives, and continue to bless us. Knowing all that I knew regarding God and his blessings, I could not understand why I could not seem to trust him for everything in my life. I felt that God needed assistance to direct my path. God doesn't need any help from anyone. He knows everything about me, down to the number of follicles I have in my head. The problem was with me, I felt that God wasn't moving fast enough to bring about changes in my life. So I felt it was my duty to help things along. Well, you guessed it. I tried and fell flat on my face. God proved to me that I needed him, and not the other way around.

The devil had me right where he wanted me to be. I was looking for a man to end the loneliness that I was feeling instead of looking to God to fill that void. I was taken in by the sweet words that were being spoken to me, as well as the infrequent dates that I went on. I was in a desperate state of mind, and I took the least amount of attention that I received from the men in my life to mean that they truly loved me. I wasn't used to receiving compliments from the opposite sex, so when I did get them, I took it to mean something that it wasn't. Well, of course, I was very wrong in my assumption. I should have remembered that God is a jealous God, and that we shall have no other above him. God wants his children to be happy and have a spouse as he clearly states in Exodus 20:3 (KJV). *"Thou shalt have no other God's before me."* This is one of the most important of the Ten Commandments given to Moses by God. Just to clarify what that means: if we put anyone or anything above glorifying, obeying, praising, or worshiping God, he will remove it from our lives, for he is a jealous God.

14

Out of Control

On August 30, 2014, my life took a turn that would end up being the start of a downward spiral. First, I received news that the company I was employed with at the time had decided to fire me for taking a lunch break away from the client's home. The company tried to say I didn't follow their policy. Well, God was still in my corner. The unemployment specialist in charge of my case informed the company that I was allowed to take a lunch break away from the place of business, or else they would have to pay me as if I had a working lunch. I received unemployment for thirty-six weeks, and the company ended up having to close all their Georgia locations. Although I was granted unemployment, I was put in a very difficult financial situation. I was accustomed to having a monthly income of five figures; and now I was bringing in $245 per week.

I applied for various jobs, but I remained unemployed. After thirty-six weeks, the unemployment benefits ended, and there I was with no income at all. I couldn't believe what was happening to my life now. Here I was, a nurse with two associate degrees, two bachelor degrees, and two master's degrees—and I couldn't find a job. All I could do was cry and get depressed. There was no one to help me, absolutely no one. I remember going to my mother and crying as I told her, "I have nothing. I have literally lost everything that I had—no job, no car, no income at all." I felt completely alone and lost. I remember lying on the floor and finally crying out, "God, I have absolutely nothing anymore. I have completely made a mess of my life, please help me." Then I heard a quiet voice say to me, "Now I can use you. I have emptied you, and now I can rebuild you into the woman you were destined to be."

I had to learn that God was my source for everything and not depend on anyone or anything to provide for me. I started studying the Bible and reconnecting with God. I went back to praying with a sincere heart. He directed me to read various scriptures. One in particular was Philippians 4: 19 (KJV). *"But my God shall supply all your needs according to his riches in glory by Christ Jesus."*

Approximately two weeks later, I was praying, and the Lord spoke to me again. This time he told me to go to the Salvation Army. At first, I thought, *How could I have let this happen that I need to seek the Salvation Army for help?* I didn't understand, but I obeyed God's instructions. What I couldn't see at the time was how God was using my current situation to help me get rid of my pride and prideful thinking. I went to the Salvation Army, and I was given food stamps. One of the counselors came to my house to do an evaluation, to see what other assistance I needed. After the evaluation, she sent me to a money management class. Upon completion of the class, I was sent back to the counselor for guidance. I didn't know God was doing me favor and working things out for me.

The next day, the counselor called me to inform me that the Salvation Army was going to pay my mortgage for the past amount due and for the next two months. They also paid my utilities in the same manner. I was very shocked regarding what was just explained to me. I never even thought to seek help from them. God wanted me to see how people that were less fortunate than me, or those who fell on tough times survived. It was so clear to me how at any given time we all may be one paycheck away from being homeless.

The Salvation Army paid a total of $6,250 for my bills that I didn't have the resources to pay. At that very moment, I was humbled by God. Despite everything that I had done wrong, God was still providing for me, blessing me, and granting me a favor. I would go to the grocery store and find expensive meat with the wrong prices, and the store had to give it to me for the price shown. One day I went to the store and found a 12-pound prime rib packaged for $3.25. I couldn't believe my eyes. All I could say was, "Thank you, Jesus." Because he allowed us to find numerous deals and we were able to stock our freezer from bottom to top with the amount of stamps I was receiving. God showed up and showed out just for me.

Approximately a week later, I was offered a job as a night janitor for one of the local colleges at night making $8 an hour. I put all pride aside again and gladly accepted the job. I made the decision to follow God's lead this time. I immediately started mailing my tithes to the church. I was able to get off food the stamps, but I still didn't have a car. I kept that job faithfully for three months, and then God blessed me with a job that paid $25 an hour. I continued to faithfully mail in my tithe.

One Friday afternoon, God spoke to my heart and led me to go to a car dealership. I didn't hesitate this time. When I got to the dealership, I informed the salesman that I had no credit, as I had just started a new job and my last car had been repossessed due to not having continuous employment. The salesman looked at me and asked to see my pay stub. I obliged and gave him what I had. He told me to go out to the lot and pick any car that I wanted. Of course, I was skeptical, because I couldn't afford a big payment, and I didn't have any money for a down payment.

I followed the directions of the salesman and picked out a car that I liked. Guess what, God showed me favor again. I drove off the lot with the car of my choice and didn't have to make a down payment and my monthly payment was only $340 a month. God made a way where there was no way to be seen.

From that day on, he kept blessing me with jobs that I didn't even apply for. I went from making $300 a week to making $2,500 a week. I was able to go to church on a regular basis again, sow seeds of faith, and continue paying my tithe and offerings. I was so thankful to God, I decided to give back to the Salvation Army for helping me when I needed help. I was able to go to various stores and buy clothing and personal care items, which I donated to the various shelters every month. Not only had God humbled and restored me, he showed me how to be empathetic toward his people. That is an experience I will never take for granted.

15

Self-Realization

My life was good, and I was serving God like I desired, going to church faithfully, studying my Bible more, and enjoying my jobs. There was only one problem. I forgot about Matthew 26:41, where God clearly tells us to *"watch as and pray, that ye enter not into temptation: the spirit indeed is willing but the flesh is weak."* I let my guard down and was giving money to the man I was involved with and came to care for deeply. I thought I was doing something good to keep him happy. Problem number 1: God didn't bless me to turn around and place man above him again. Later, I found out that the money I was giving him, well, he was spending it and his time with another woman. I don't blame him for what happened. I was totally to blame because I knew better. Women, always remember: if a man wants to be with you, then he will do everything for you and not the other way around. It was a painful lesson to learn, and I began to fall into a deep depression again.

The day before my birthday, I was so preoccupied while driving that I didn't realize I was speeding. I had forgotten that I didn't have my insurance because I had used the money for something else. Well, I was pulled over, and fear immediately took over; and I gave the officers a different name than my name. I was hoping I could just pay the ticket and that would be the end of it, but I was so very wrong. Well, as we all know, what is done in secret will eventually come out. When I went to pay the ticket, I was told that I had to produce my license. Well, that was impossible because I gave a different name. So by then, the person was notified of the ticket; and needless to say, she was very upset with me. I tried to pay the ticket, but that wasn't going to be enough for them. I asked for forgiveness, but they weren't willing to accept my apology or forgive me at the time.

I had just started a new job working from home when two officers came to my house and arrested me for giving a false name. To my surprise, I wasn't upset or crying. I figured if God was letting me to go to jail, then there had to be a reason. The officer who came to arrest me was the same officer I gave the false name to. Both officers were polite and waited until a family member came to my house to care for my mom. They took me out to the car but did not put me in handcuffs.

As the officer was driving the car I called out to him and told him how sorry I was for giving him a false name. He accepted my apology and stated, "You seem to be a good person. You care for your mom and work from home, don't beat yourself up about this at all. We all do stupid things at some point in our life. I will tell the judge that I think you just made the wrong choice but that deep down, you are a good person."

During the long ride, all I could do was thank Jesus for all he had done for me. You may think it's crazy, but I didn't. I looked at the situation as an honor that God was about to use me for his glory. Once we got to the jail, one of the nurses there recognized me and told the officer I was a diabetic and needed to stay down in that particular area (God's favor). I was fingerprinted, and the officer told me not to worry because even though it was a holiday weekend, they were having a bond hearing that Saturday morning, and I wasn't going to have to be there till Tuesday (God's favor). I was then placed in the holding area with five other women. I started praying, "Okay, God, what is my assignment?" I was reminded of one of my bishop's sermons entitled "Golden Connections." Never let an encounter be treated lightly. With that in mind, I was ready to complete the assignment God had placed before me.

Well, the first young lady asked me why I was in jail, because it was clear to her that I didn't belong there. I told her I was there because of something I had done over a year ago and now it was my time to answer for it. She began to explain to me that she was there on a drug charge, but that she wasn't aware of drugs being in the car. I thought, *Okay, Lord, what will you have me say to her, or what do you want me to do?* I began to tell the young lady that she needed to be more careful and think seriously about the company she was keeping. I also told her that she was still young enough to turn her life around once she was released from jail this time. I told her how much God loved her no matter what she had done in her past, and that if she was ready to make a change in her life, God was there and willing to accept her as his child and change the course of her life. She sat for a moment and looked at me, and then she politely said, "Thank you."

The guard brought two more women to the holding area that had been arrested for prostitution. One of the young ladies began to cry because she was informed that they were not entitled to a bond because they actually lived in South Carolina. I looked at both of the young ladies and saw that they were, in fact, very beautiful. I asked both of them, was it worth it now being in jail and away from their children? One of the young ladies said that it was her child's birthday and now she was going to miss the whole event. The other young lady said to me, "What do you know about selling your body for money?" I politely told the young lady that in my younger years, I gave my body to a man once, hoping that I would make him love me, but instead, I was a participant in sexual acts that I despised. She looked at me and said, "You look so mature and well put together." I told her looks can be very deceiving.

As our conversation continued, I asked them both what they wanted to do with their life instead of what they were doing now. They both informed me that they wanted to go to school to make a better life for themselves and their children. I told them both that God loved them just as they were, but they had to first love themselves enough to see that they deserved a lifestyle that would make them happy and their children safe. I preceded to tell them that if they wanted to make a change in their life, all they had to do was pray to God to forgive them of their sins, and then just watch him move and make a way for them where there seemed to be no way.

One of the young ladies said to me, "If God is so good like you say he is, then why are you here in jail?" I told the young lady that I was God's servant and that he trusted me and wanted me here "to be a witness to you, young ladies." I also told them that sometimes God will allow tests and trials to come into our lives to grow us in Christ. I told them I felt honored that God trusted me enough for this particular assignment. Both ladies were surprised by my response.

By this time, they called my name for me to be processed in so I left the holding cell. Once I was at the station with the guard, I saw an old friend from high school who just happened to be a bondsman (God working). He called to me, "Lil' Kid, is that you?" I replied, "Yes, it is me." He told me not to worry, that he would have a bond hearing the next day and he would take my case on (God's favor). I was surprised because I had not even made a phone call for a bond. He proceeded to take my information, the name of my family member to call, and then he would handle the rest.

After I was processed, I was taken upstairs for the night. I was able to call my mom to assure her that I was all right and would speak to her in the morning. There wasn't a Bible in the room where they put me, but I was all right. You see, that's the wonderful thing about prayer and reading your Bible when you can. The Lord was with me as he brought back to my spirit the many scriptures that I had been studying. I walked around the cell, praying and praising God until I fell asleep.

I was awakened by the nurse calling my name to have my blood sugar checked before breakfast was served. I was then taken to another holding cell for my bond hearing. By this time, I felt revitalized after spending that much-needed quiet time with God. I began to speak to the Lord in my spirit, saying, "Okay, Lord, what is my assignment for today?"

Just then, another young lady was brought into the holding cell where I was waiting. Suddenly she blurted out, "I'm here because I tried to kill my neighbor."

I thought, Okay, God, what do I say to this one?

The Lord softly spoke to my spirit. *Just listen to her, and then you will know what to say.*

So that's what I did. I just listened.

She shouted, "It's all his fault!" Then she began to cry. She told me that she had invested all her money into buying her house and that her neighbor had been messing with her since the first day she moved into the house. She told me he would destroy her belongings, come to her property, and take things and cause her pure hell every day. She then said, "I am a Christian, and I pay my tithes faithfully, but enough was enough." She told me she took her bat and hit her neighbor in his knees, breaking both legs. She continued to hit him all over from his chest and arms, until the other neighbors pulled her away from him. By now, she was up pacing in the holding cell and clinching her fist.

I quietly spoke to her. "May I ask you a question?" She nodded yes. I said, "No offense, but did you ever stop to pray for your neighbor?"

She looked at me as if I had two heads and said, "No."

I continued with our conversation and said to her, "Didn't you think that if you prayed to God to help your neighbor and give him peace in his life, then he wouldn't be bothering you?" I explained to her that if she had indeed prayed for God to comfort him in whatever was bothering him, then he wouldn't have taken his pain and frustrations out on her.

The young lady looked at me and began to cry. She was suddenly filled with remorse and began to pray to God to forgive her and for her neighbor to be all right. After she calmed down, she looked at me and said, "I don't know what you did to be in here, but God sent you to me."

All I could do was give her a hug and whisper, "I agree with you completely."

It was now time for me to go before the judge. The process took thirty minutes for him to grant me a bond. We walked out of the courtroom, and I started to ask the guard if I could make a phone call to get released. Just as I looked up I saw my high school friend. He came over to me and said, "Don't worry, I got you all taken care of, and you will be out in no time at all." (God's favor.)

We were taken back upstairs to the general population. I was walking and talking to God and thanking him for the opportunity to witness to the women I came in contact with. By now, I was ready to go home; but an hour had passed and I was still there. I began to talk to God again, and I said, "God, what part of my assignment haven't I completed?"

At that moment, I heard a voice that I thought I recognized. I rushed to the window, and sure enough, it was the voice of a homeless woman that I had met over six months ago. I hadn't seen her in a few months, and I was getting a little concerned regarding her welfare. I met her one day as I was going to get some coffee. My spirit was drawn to her, and I bought her some breakfast, and we sat in the middle of a huge parking lot and talked for what seemed to have been for hours. I learned she was from a prominent family in Savannah, but she was diagnosed with schizophrenia and she became homeless because of the ups and downs of her condition. I tried to convince her to go to a shelter, but she said they were not safe. Over the next several months, I would pray for her and for the Lord to let me see her often to provide whatever she needed at the time. She was so sweet, and she instilled in me an immense amount of knowledge. I was able to reconnect her with her sister, and every time I saw her, I would let her use my phone to talk with her. Her sister had been reaching out to me, asking if I knew where she was; but I had no idea where to find her. At that moment, I looked up and said, "Lord, now I see why I am still here. I can give her sister the good news about her condition." Just then, the guard called my name, and I was soon released.

When I got outside, my aunt was waiting for me. I then received a phone call from my best friend, who was also waiting for me. I called my best friend and apologized for causing him any embarrassment; but he just said he was just happy that I was okay. I then called my son, who was also just happy I was doing okay. The next person that I called was the man I had been seeing at the time. He simply told me that he would never judge me that way, because we all make mistakes, and he really thought I was in one of my moods again and not wanting to talk to him, but he was glad I was doing okay as well.

The next person I called was the sister of the homeless woman. I told her that her sister was in jail, but that she looked good and she was taking her medications. She was so happy to hear the news because she feared that her sister was dead. I was happy to give her peace of mind. The final person I called was my pastor, Bishop S. O. Bulloch, to inform him of what had happened. Of course, people had already called and told him where I was that weekend. In his so soft and loving voice, he said, "I had already called our church secretary and informed her that she knew what needed to be done." To my surprise, I had five people waiting to pay my bond. (God's favor.)

I was glad to be home, and even more excited to relay to my bishop the assignment that God had given me, and how I was able to complete it. God allowed me to be put in jail for twenty-four hours while he used me to witness and connect with five different women that needed him at that time.

The Sunday following my release from jail, I was at a restaurant with my mother, and I saw one of the women who was in jail with me. She saw me and immediately bowed her head and began to walk in the other direction. I caught up with her and told her how happy I was to see her, and then I asked her, why did she look at me and then turn to go the other way?

She simply said, "You look so nice in your church clothes, I thought you wouldn't want anyone to know that you knew me, or how we actually met."

I immediately gave her a big hug and pulled her over to the table where my mother was sitting and introduced her. I told her that I didn't care where I was, that if she saw me, she was always welcome to greet me because I wasn't ashamed to know her.

She then had a big smile on her face and said, "I took your advice, and I moved into my own apartment. I have a new job, and I was just coming from church myself."

I said, "Look at God."

I gave her my card and told her that if she ever needed anything, she was welcome to call me. She gave me a big hug and said, "You are the real deal, a true Christian."

As I look back on this experience, I am reminded of Paul and his experience as described in Philippians 1:18–20.

> *What then? Notwithstanding every way, whether in pretense, or in truth, Christ is preached: and I there in do rejoice, yea, and will rejoice. For I know that this shall turn to my salvation through your prayer, and the supply of the spirit of Jesus Christ. According to my earnest expectation and my hope, that in nothing I shall be ashamed, but with all boldness, as always, so now also Christ shall be magnified in my body, whether it be by life, or by death.*

16

Getting on Track

The entire experience reminded me of my Bishop S. O. Bulloch's sermon entitled, "How Are You Going through Your Storm?" It put things into perspective for me. Think about it for a moment. When we have our storms, do we groan, grumble, and complain, or do we forget about our problems and help someone else? It's when we can help others that God will bless us. As Christians, we are reminded of this very thing in 1 Peter 4:12–13. *"Beloved, think it not strange concerning the fiery trial which is to try you, as though some strange thing happened unto you. But rejoice, inasmuch as yea are partakers of Christ's sufferings; that when his glory shall be revealed, ye may be glad also with exceeding joy."*

I was very humbled that God was able to trust me to carry out his assignment. If we give our will over to God, there is nothing he won't do for us. Matthew 18:18 decrees, *"Truly, I say unto you, whatever you bind on earth shall be bound in heaven, and whatever you loose on earth shall be loosed in heaven."* He will give you your heart's desire.

I remember on two different occasions how the Lord comforted me and gave me what I had asked him for. I was feeling so alone and unloved one afternoon. I spoke to the Lord and simply said, "Lord, I know you love me, and I know you are there for me, but my physical body just needs a hug." At that very moment, I heard a knock on the car window, and it was my son. I was surprised, because at the time, he was living in Jacksonville, Florida, because he was in the navy and it was on a weekday. I opened the car door, and he just stood there with his arms stretched out to hold me. All I could say was, "Thank you, God. You knew I needed that hug." I asked my son what he was doing home in the middle of the week, and he simply said, "I had a feeling you needed me, so I took off early to come see you."

On another occasion, I was feeling down and alone because I was missing my father very badly. Again, I spoke to God and said, "I'm feeling so alone right now. My father is gone, and I don't have a husband to turn to for comfort."

Just then, a song came over the radio, and it was CeCe Winans. I thought, *I have all of her CD's but I had never heard this song before.* The name of the song was "Never Have to Be Alone." I was so touched by the words of the song that I cried and said, "God, you had this song to play at this very moment just for me, and it was everything I was feeling."

Well, I tried to look up the song to download it, but I found out that the CD wasn't due out for another three months. It was at that moment that I knew for a fact that God hears our pain, and if we ask him, then he will provide the comfort and peace that we need.

17

Acceptance

Philippians 1:6 decrees, *"Being confident of this very thing, that he which hath begun a good work in you will perform it until the day of Jesus Christ."*

Looking back over this stage of my life, I can see how God had his hands in every situation I was in. My pastor, Bishop S. O. Bulloch, preached a sermon one Tuesday evening at Bible study. He said, "It's a process. God has to work some things out of you while working some things in to you." God wants the best for his children; and at the same time, he wants us to share his word, works, and love for everyone.

We have all experienced our own up-and-down cycle in life. When God blesses us and everything is good, we tend to stop with our praise and worship for him. But when everything is in shambles and we are in trouble, we run to God and fall on our knees and plead for his help. As Christians, we need to be consistent in our praise and worship and obey God at all times. 1 Thessalonians 5:18 states, *"In everything give thanks: for this is the will of God in Christ Jesus concerning you."* I have learned to trust God with the big problems in my life, but thought I could handle the small things. God wants it all—he is our Lord, our Savior, and we must glorify and revere him as the Lord of Lords and King of Kings. In the words of my bishop, "Lord, keep me humble." It's when we stay humbled before him that he can, and will do everything he said he will do because *"God is not a man that he should lie, neither the son of man, that he should repent: hath he said, and hall not do it? Or hath he spoken, and shall he not make it good?"* (Num. 23:19)

For this very reason, we are assured that God should be first in our life. He will never deceive us or forsake us. God's love for us was shown when he performed the greatest sacrifice for our sins. Yes, just as we do sometimes, God had a moment when he questioned completing his assignment. This can be found in Luke 22:42, where he said, *"Father if thou be willing, remove this cup from me: Nevertheless not my will, but thine, be done."* So he laid down his life so that we may have everlasting life with him. The only thing he asks of us is to obey him, serve him, treat others the way he would treat them, and spread the gospel of Jesus Christ.

You may think, Well, if God was all that, then why did I do the things that I did?

Well, I have learned that God is in control of our lives. He knows our end at the beginning. Even though some things I caused to come upon myself because of disobedience, God had the power to stop everything that I was doing wrong, but that's not how God works. He wants us to come to him as a willing vessel, and he will use every action, mistake, decision we make to direct our lives. Remember, God is the alpha and omega; and for that reason alone, I love him and give my life willingly to him to be used for his glory.

God Bless.

About the Author

Tanya Kidd believes that through Christ all things are possible. Tanya stepped out on faith and answered God's call to write her first novel, but certainly not her last. Born in Aberdeen, Maryland, and raised in El Paso, Texas, and Savannah, Georgia, Tanya is a clinical nurse specialist by profession. Tanya has one child, Petty Officer 2nd Class Timothy Kidd. Timothy currently resides in Virginia Beach, Virginia, with his wife and children. In addition to her new literary career, Tanya is also CEO/owner of Caring Hearts of Savannah, LLC, and Anything Nursing, LLC. Tanya is currently single and resides in Savannah. You can find her on Facebook and Twitter @TanyaKidd10.

CPSIA information can be obtained
at www.ICGtesting.com
Printed in the USA
LVHW09s1303310818
588790LV00001B/41/P